100 Poems

Till Lindemann

Translated by Tom Dybel

RAW DOG
SCREAMING
PRESS

Published by Raw Dog Screaming Press
Bowie, MD

Cover Motive and interior illustrations: © Matthias Matthies
Author Photo: Bryan Adams

Printed in the United States of America

ISBN: 978-1-947879-96-6 / 978-1-947879-97-3

Library of Congress Control Number: 2021930718

www.RawDogScreaming.com

With illustrations from
Matthias Matthies

Contents

Music

Loneliness is a concert
a din roaring out of my gullet
the fiddles screeching charmingly
the harps sneaking into my flesh
a voice leaping out of my mouth
sings ferociously into my ear
the kettledrum crashes frenziedly
against the gates of my soul

By the Beach

By the beach by the beach
Sits a man with a hard on
On a fence
And his hard on is plain
To see

What's he up to what's he up to
He's looking at the girls
They're nude
He's old
He gets hot
They get cold
He is up to
Rubbing himself
A public off-fence
Indeed

Captain

Where's the captain gone
Nowhere to be seen
Can't see anyone
Water in the way
Water all around
We're going to go down
What a holiday

Money

Who knows how long our love will last
I love you you love my credit card

Mine

Seems bound
To your little heart no more
Its sound its beat obeys
A different unfamiliar score

Apart from your pulse
And from you
It trips up on its own blood
An alien throbbing through

Beats frail
And lonely falter
Memories as pale
As washing up water

A heart that knows
What it truly wants to do
Flies off like a thieving crow
And vehemently seeks to be close to you

Quiet

I love music
But I like it quiet
My ears can't bear
The din the blare
Quiet cozy let it be
Loud is agony for me

Rowdy

I'm a genuine rowdy
I break all the rules
Whatever I want I do
And the fun's just getting rougher
I do what I have to do
Treat men and women cruel
To make the whole world suffer
Agony for all and none I spare
Except animals
Yeah

Time Out

I had time she needed dough
So what do you think I asked
Sure enough quick as a flash
She didn't give me no no
So she had dough
I needed time
Empty pocket no beer no toot
Had to get back home on foot

And They're Calling Out to Me

They are calling they are screaming
Put us in your mouth for your pleasure
At your leisure we wait
My appetite's not that great
But their screams are unbearable
They howl so terrible
All we want want want is you
So so luscious we will taste
You'll be licking us off your finger-us
Give us oh give us to your face
Tip us out the pan onto the plate

Their insistence weakens my resistance
As always
With spaghetti bolognese

No Heart

Soon we'll again be not united
so many tears not cried
Strong arms lovely thighs
but no eyes
When I cry
And no heart neither

The Guilty One is Me of Course

It's very clear to see
Wordlessly I scream
I speak truth when I lie
Honestly try to deceive
I mourn my youth has passed
The years are passing away
Got no bird in the hand
No bird in the bush will stay
I have to kiss you
Have to feel you
Want to hold you
Want to touch you
Have to breathe you
Talk with you
And
I want to praise you
Have to punish you
Lie with you
Sleep with you
But as every day goes past
I can't ignore your hideous
Non-stop viciousness
Loving you's no fun I've just
Put up with you for long enough
Owing guilt to guiltiness
But I'll lighten up the gloom
When I lie I speak the truth
I can't ignore you're hideous
The guilty one is me of course

Post

My tears to send
Address below a dress
Our fucking's had to end
Sender is sadness
My heart's heaviness
Happy everyone else
Having a Christmastime
O tree o Tannenbaum
Your dress
Is going up in flame

Chain

All alone
So alone
He wanted to die
When a dog came by
And gave him love
That pup
Saved his life
So he chained it up

Licking

When I'm licking her legs
I drool
A snail
Trail
Gummy slobber goo
Some boy dew joins to
My drool
Heading home
When her legs I'm licking
Beathing in this fume pure
I wouldn't be
Anywhere but here

I'm talking

About this and that
Talking on and on and on
Asking this and asking that…
Does fucking really turn you on?

Nasty look from her

I'm only trying to be nice to you
Trying to be your verbal slave
There's nothing that I want to get from you
I'm only here to entertain

And all at once hey ho it's in
That's not so bad now is it quim
Shit happens no need to be shy
And the night's so dark intent is blind
Yet still gets what it's got in mind
So who's to blame—not you
Nor your pussy so fine to screw
Nor me—the one to be convicted
Is my penis he is so wicked and anyway
If you hadn't been sucking him
I'd not have stuck him in

25

Autobahn

They left me under a bridge
And never came back for me
They drove away towards the south
Don't even know my name
Don't know how old I am
Don't know when my first tooth
They never came back for me
Born on the autobahn

Ingrate

An insect fell into the waves
And nearly drowned how nice I am
I cupped my hand beneath it saved
The creature's life but damn it stang
Me stupid ingrate what a pain

Poor Bear

The poor bear's dead
In his blood's warmth
His brown
Shoulder, pelt, gone inside
Outside
Red lost
Both arms
The machete chopped away
No more the bear can pray

The poor bear no arms

By his little cot the child
Also soon dead
Can't even bleed
Cannot grasp
just like the bear
lost both arms
The machete chopped away
Wouldn't pray with mother today

The poor child of arms

Dance of Death

Give me give me echoes
Round the room
Blowing chilly
On your lips red foam tied a label to your toe
Nothing's able to hurt you

Testicles slacken, by the hair
I hold you to control my desire
Never again I wanted to
Not wanting to you want it too

To water my lawn
Let your tears flow please
The lid dam bursts
The skin tree drinks
Of you
Be afraid
Red foam
Lucky fear
A cold wind
Echoes round the room

On your toe a label
I pinch you hard
I'm unable
To make you hurt
Stretched on the table
You keep me cold
You remain inert

Even when my foot
Is on the label
Your blue toes

Not My Wife

I love my wife so strong
I love her no denying
Yes everything's just fine
Except that far too long
The same one has been mine

Conjugal duty what a bore
A change is as good as a rest
With her it's a dreadful chore
If only she were someone else

I know her far too well
Too long she's been my wife
My next door neighbour's wife
Now that would sure be nice

Great figure lovely face
But my wife no siree
This wife of mine no way
I'd rather watch TV

Total Loss

Take a good look that bag of sleaze
What a stinking eyesore jeez
Never keeps his bumcrack clean
Cruddy whiff from funky cheeks
Sweat's soaked deep into his jeans
From mouldy crotch down to the knees
Armpits silted up with rot
Hooker's cots for lice and fleas
Etched into his feet his socks
And topping off
The total loss of self-respect
Reeking round the block
The unwashed cock

Love

Wait wait I'm really into you
Heart and gold and stars I'll give you
Fire burns within my rib cage
Love they call it if inanely
Crumple up your pretty soul
Toss it on the happy flame
Soon everything goes up in smoke
Only ashes will remain

Victim of Art

Mister Peter Pelham Swithin
Was a poet to poetry married
Everywhere he went he carried
Luxury pen and paper with him

Even on a cycling tour
He oftentimes would stop and jot
Down his thoughts he thought a lot
Of thoughts that from his brain did pour

He simply stopped this was his habit
Any time a rhyme occurred
In the middle of the road
Hindering the other traffic

Criticised he changed his mode of
Fixing every inspiration
Wrote without deceleration
And the handlebar let go of

What happened next
Surely everyone's guessed
Hands free faster and faster
Scrawling verses possibly his best
Crashed at last and met disaster
Killing himself with a pen through his chest

Skinhate

The skinhate has an alien style
Far at the horizon he seeks his heil
Sticks his arm straight out and ever more so
Until it falls right off his torso

Town and Country

In every town are girls
Pigtails and charms
Running through the streets
Ringing our alarms
In every town some guy
Is always fighting someone
Often because of girls
Sometimes because of women
That'll be why
People prefer the countryside
But it's no better there
As the name implies

Witch

What have I done
What did I not do
What witch
Will nurse this curse

The Sad People's Army

Are you sad as sad as me
Tears are running down your face
Come and join our company
Come and join our sad brigade

Why be lonely sniveling
Join our ranks be one of us
March with us in misery
One for all and all for one

Come now join our company
None should weep alone alone
Solitary suffer woe
Join the army of the low

We're the ugly and the gross
Chuckers tongue their bitter pills
Cutters wave their razor blades
Saddos joined for better ills

Joyless marching joylessly
All endure one agony
Singing in a minor key
A heavy song and no tee-hee

When we join our sadnesses
We help the pain to bear a child

When we weep together then
For the child the sun might shine

Early Mass

Twas in the merry merry month of May
But the snow and ice all around did lay
Beside me in the church my darling knelt
And shivered and froze my heart to melt

Thereupon her trembling hand did I feel
Behind me as by her side did I kneel
With a hesitant look most carefully she
Shoved her fist up inside my arse cavity

Must you my darling I did exclaim
Whereupon she gently did explain
Warm wrists make the blood warm everywhere
And a warm heart makes for warmer prayers

Small

Small fingers
Small bosoms
Small he
Small apples
Small fingers
Touch me

Apple

An apple is a well known food
Both tastes good and is good for you
but one thing does not win applause
the noise it makes between your jaws

When Your Mother Died

When your mother died
What a lovely time
You looked at me so sad the way
That makes me swell
My lust it drove me mad
I hope she goes to hell

When your mother died
You kissed me so intense
Yhe way that makes me swell
Overwhelmed my senses
I hope she goes to hell

When your mother died
You wept so many tears
I hugged you and stroked
And pretty soon my dear
We fucked like goats

When your mother died
Such a lovely time
My life I'd pay
To see your mother
Go to hell every day

Alone

Another dawn the rising sun
God's kindergarten tainted red
I load a bullet in the gun but
I'm afraid to shoot me dead

I'm all alone once more
My heart can't lonely die
I never wanted to be born
I never asked to be alive

I'm always so alone
I'll always be alone
If someone would take aim at me
I'd take a bullet and be free

What ...

You're out upon the wild waters
I can't see you, night-blind
Running up and down the shore
Call your name into the wind

Why not come back to shore
No one admits how cold they feel
Swam out far too far
What was it brought us here

I sent a signal up for you
So you'd find me easily
The flare illuminates the night
But it doesn't shine on me

But hope's got nothing to hold onto
Salt swallowing gale tossed
On the shore soaked and freezing
You don't care if I'm lost

Preparation

There's something I've been preparing
Hey scaredy
Eyes stark staring
I've
You've
We've got company
So different everything's going to be
She three comes out of the bathroom declaring
There's something I've been preparing

Summer

Summer's come and gobbled May
All our worries yesterday
But no peace now for a man
Already all the grief began

Sunshine lights up women's skin
Naked patches brightly swim
Dazzling in my eyes' delight
Hurt my tongue and scrotum tight

Spring's been eaten up by March
Sunbathe in a woman's heart
Sting the brain and creep in veins
Siren songs make me insane

Thousand needlepricks of urge
To let me get my hands on her
Generous flesh I want to seize
Oh feel them giving way my knees

Helplessly I have to look on
As they let their babies suck on
What so gently bounces, quivers
Siren songs give me the shivers

Crawling in toward my groin
Other sexes scents to join
Lash me to the mast and blind
Fold me please and I won't mind

Siren songs I'm still their prey
Must try to lean my mind away
But justifying my worst fears
Lust comes pouring out my ears

Fine Weather

Lovely weather out today
I prefer it terrible
Sunshine makes people nice and kind
Perfectly unbearable

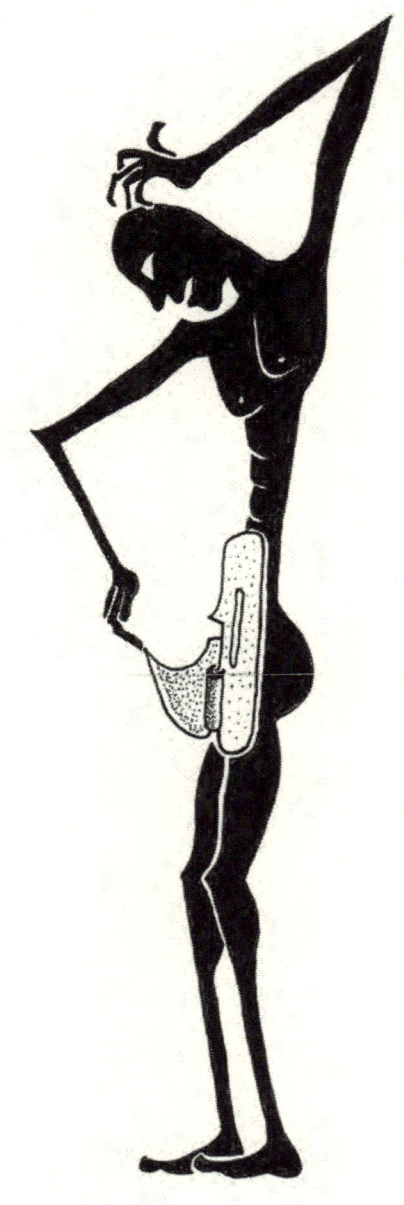

52

I Was Hungry

So I went into the shed and fetched the bow
The roebuck was standing square behind the hydrangeas looking
    distrustfully over at us
In next door's garden a children's birthday party was going on
    and we were afraid
The screaming might make the horned beast leap away
So wait
We stayed quiet, so did the children, and he went back to grazing
The animal paused at the end of the garden so I had to steal
    closer to get a good shot
I'd loaded a sharpened bolt and crawled over the lawn
Various thoughts were passing through my head
I need to get bacon so the meat won't dry out in the oven
Cream for the sauce there must be some in the fridge and
    cranberries yeah none left
But the neighbours'll lend me some
Venison without cranberries no way
I tensed my bow, drew the bowstring up to the tip of my nose
Took aim
The moment I let it fly the kids next door started singing
Happy Birthday and the buck leapt up
The bolt smacked into the animal's kidneys and hung there
With a scream that went right through me and its back bent
The little buck hurtled through the flower beds, sprang over the
    fence and fled
Straight into the birthday party

In our part of town the roe deer population has swelled
    enormously in recent years

The animals get into gardens and lawns, even into greenhouses and
parks where they eat everything that smells and looks good
No one's allowed to hunt them
So there are more and more of them

Screaming
Plates smashed onto the ground we heard crying women's voices
shouting their children's names and Don't touch it
I ran to the cool room grabbed the fillet knife and followed by two
of my friends who were also hungry we leapt over the fence
One of the lads tore his trousers
Outside the house next door a macabre vision
The buck was standing head bowed in front of the swimming pool
bleeding
And giving out screams
Like a newborn baby
Some children were standing crying and staring at him
Others were running round the garden sobbing loudly to themselves
and over and over again we heard Mama and No
The mothers were standing under the party canopy paralysed
with fear calling out their offspring's names
Which you couldn't make out amid the din
I sat down on a chair with the deboner in my hand and shouted
into the din that there was no need to worry
This was a perfectly normal hunting incident I'd got everything under
control and the animal would soon be put out of its misery
More howls, more screaming, I crept closer with the blade towards
the bleeding creature to finish it off
Followed by my mate with the ripped trousers under which you
could now see his grey underwear
I leapt at the animal's legs to bring it down but
In mortal fear with his last strength the buck got up and made one

great leap in among the floating balls and inflatable swans
Into the pool
Gurgling and gasping he tried to stay on the surface
Making sounds reminiscent of sea lions
But finally sank while still very slowly carrying on making swimming
    motions
The kids stared at one another
The mothers were screaming at me to do something and waving
    cake forks around
I leapt at the animal
We dragged our meal out of the water and it was very weak and so
I was able to get my cold weapon into its life and quickly it was over
The twitching ceased the screaming stopped and hysteria gave
way to rubber-necking
The kids stared at the kill puffy eyed from crying but interested
    in what we were carrying home on our backs
The man of the house now came up to me
He was wearing a colourful apron calling him Chef of the Day
    and carrying barbecue tongs
Which he threatened to use on me and to call the police
I threatened him back with my bow said I'd use it on him and
    the children and the police could do nothing anyway
Soon after we ate
He had no cranberries
I didn't feel like asking the other neighbours
It was quiet over there and we weren't hungry anymore

Animal Migration

Can be from plate to mouth
Plants stand patiently and true
Firmly rooted in the earth
Vegetables are good for you

Animal migration
Deer and cows we eat
And sing a celebration
But no one's paying the least attention

Animal migration
Happens universally
Plate to mouth migration
Chewing has to be
Or else they might flee

Animal migration
Is right for them and me and you
No trial or tribulation
But plants stand patiently and true
They are excluded from the rule

Animal migration
More to say there's not a lot
The noise they make deserves ovation
People sing and plants do not

Animal migration
You mustn't oh it mustn't be

With angelic orchestration
You shall not kill—the proclamation

People do eat veal
Lions do eat wildebeest
They all keep singing
But no one's paying the least attention

Farewell to a Beloved Animal

And Christmas again already
How fast the time ...

We took him into the bathroom
He wasn't lookng good
And we sort of felt sorry for him
After all you spent a lot of time with the creature
And get used to it especially the children
I tried to comfort them said he was just old
We laid him in the tub and
I started running the taps
Our daughter started crying
I tried to comfort her said he likes water
The wife shook her head and said I should
Put an end to it the animal was suffering in pain
And anyway she didn't have all day
The silver needed polishing and Schmutzli Anti-Santa
    was on his way

Everything had to be ready
I fetched a meat mallet both children started wailing
I tried to comfort them said it would be better for him
    or something
I hit him once
Hard
Sounded like stepping on an egg
No blood a lot of thrashing so I slit from arse to neck
Pulled everything out
Hell of a mess a twitching and gurgling

The children screamed and then suddenly
Quiet
It was all over a sob and two rolls of kitchen paper later
I hung the bleeder on a hook
The rest was routine watched my father do it
The wife knows what to do too
Boil down and don't forget salt
At the table then they pipe up all's well again
The boy said it tasted good and he'd stopped feeling sad
The daughter smiled through drying tears fat cheeks
    and smacked her lips
The wife tousled their hair
I was lost in thoughts
I don't want any new dog

(Hong Kong 2006)

A Moor

A moor a moor
Out there a naked man
Amour amour
What is it all for
What's the naked man
Doing out on moorland
He's looking for amour
Butt naked in the boggy pits
Since amour can't be found
He's most dispirited

Love is bubbling in the mud
Thought the naked man and ran
Out to feel her skin and blood
Now he's such an angry man
See him squatting in the marsh
Sticking out a bare rump
Wanting love to bite his arse
If she rises from the swamp

Give it up man
Oh beware
Anyone can
Lose their
Life in the love moorass

You Don't Want to Know

You don't want to know
What I'm thinking
We stand together
You've a really pretty face
Awkwardly I'm twisting
And I somehow can't
Look you in the eyes

You must not know
What I'm thinking
Even if I show interest
You've such a pretty face
But what I'm really thinking is
Not for you to know

You don't want to know
What I'm thinking
Even if I'm being very nice
Making nice eyes
Just one wish is on my mind
Let me
Let me not have to beg long for this
Let me at
Let me at your whopping great tits

Cello

In the toilets at the opera house
No amount of soap can be too much
Hairs out of place she plucks out
Perfumes all her charms with graceful touch

The crowd is thrilled
The cello's chilled
Very good idea to depilate
She's a tiny bit shy
But she opens the cry
And forces the instrument to mate
Now the strings already itch
Now she'll start to air her thighs
On the bow her fingers twitch
A little sweat
The house is hushed
To hear her scent rise

Squeeze

Women aren't so hard to please
Give them skin to paw at leisure
Give them pores to pinch and squeeze
Makes the ladies weak with pleasure
Blissful, drooling they release
With fingernails deep into skin
Pus that spurts and gushes out
Blackheads bursting with a shout
Then comes a gentle groaning gasp
Lips chewed up in lust at last
Yes that's the way to spoil a gash

As always

Something lifted me up high
It felt
As if I were flying
Saw myself suddenly from above
It was great
And soon over
As always
Which isn't so great

I know that

I know the sun
The sun don't know me
It's hot when it shines
It burns into me
I know that

I know the rabbit
The rabbit knows squat
The dog gets the head
The rest's in the pot
I know that

I know my father
He knows me as well
He corporals my mother
He beats back and belly
I know that

I know people
And you know them too
They murder each other
And fly to the moon
I know that

Loneliness Again

I don't want to go home
Scared to sleep in that home
Don't want to be out alone
A boat out in a storm
When Mr Pooped scoops me up
Back to my miserable room
I'll open the shutters wide
I hate being cooped up
When the cold of night so cruel
Makes me shut the windows tight
In my loneliness so chill
I'll drench myself in fuel
Then loneliness's hug will
Squeeze me ever tighter till
Like an ape in the coil of a snake
I'll suffocate

Food

I could eat you up
Your smell and taste I adore
Oh I could devour you
Oh dear but then
You won't be there any more

Questions, Questions

Let me ask you this
Do you know why stars
Have shiny points
I do not know
Some days
They're round
Like little pearls
I do not even want to know
So many questions
A lot of people think a lot
Me I'd far
Rather stay dumb all I can say is
The stars up in the sky at night
Just the way they are
Are a lovely
Sight

On a Leash

Did you ever stop
And think
What it'd be like
To live without love
Without this shackle
Your soul's
A dog your heart brings to heel
So free your body so
Open your spirit
Different breathing
Alas no
We're all walked on that leash

Blossom

Cherry blossom on the twigs
Tulle in white the tree does kiss
Spring is on its way to us
Breathing joy into our breast
Warm days
Cold night
The beauty's plucked away by frost
Against the wall my head I smash
My days of bloom all turned to ash

When You're Asleep

I like sleeping with you when you're asleep
When you don't move in the least
Open mouth
Shut eyes
Your body there still it lies
I can touch you every part
Go crazy no holds barred
I like sleeping with you when you're dreaming
Because you're missing out on everything
And that's the way it needs to be
That way it's fun for me
A drop of rohypnol in your glass
So you can't move your arse
You asleep
I reap

Over

Dear friend let me tell you a story
I'm suffering badly indeed
I no longer know what I'm doing
She's fine and my heart bleeds

I lie down I get up from my pillow
Rats running through my chest
I go out for a walk and stay standing
Eyes open seeing nothing at best

Dear friend I would tell you a lie if
I wasn't just terrified
But I'm bravely submitting to torment
Being peeled by love's sharp knife

I'm standing but naked and heartless
She missed me she said yesterday
Our amours then discarded
Tore my life up and threw it away

It's wreckage it's shattered in pieces
You're still here and you've already gone
Everything is everything is broken
And so on and so on and so on

Each second is a whiplash
Vainly I must think of you
Must be love I must have been thinking
But no not true

Happy

I'm friendly
I say hello to everyone
I'm saying yes to life and
No to angst and gloom
Take sorrow by the hand
Though dark clouds loom

When happiness is down
I lift it off the ground
And now I have to laugh

Bat

The fluttery flutterby bat
Catched a fat gnat
And snuffed it
No joke
It must have choked
I picked it up
And stuffed it down
Yum yup

You and Your Garden

A couple called Eric and Judy
Spent most of the day in their garden
They sat sometimes on a wrought iron bench
Musing of Eden and Arden

But mostly they pottered at leisure
Together in bushes and beds
The plants that gave them most pleasure
Were roses in yellows and pinks and reds

The thornies sprang higher and higher
As Eric and Judy them nourished
Their neighbours not only admired
But envied the way they did flourish

The loveliest couple they made
Death only could prune them it seemed
Together so many a season and day
Yet something untuned them indeed

Shit happens and here shot a shoot
Of predictable midlife crisis
Led Eric to pick out younger fruit
Its taste he then found twice as nice as

Judy inside the vine arbor screamed
How much do you think I can take
Just bloody get out of the garden
But don't walk where it's been raked

Ah so many a heart gets broken this way
So many a love is doomed
If you want a lesson to take away
The roses are still in bloom

Dance Bar

Girls all act like super troopers
Cos their guys are brewers droopers.

Holidays in the Country

Summer or waking coma
that's holidays
at Grandma's (Oma)
or winter protein ration dread
out into the country for again
lumps on the back of the head

Grandpa's wife bakes us nice bread
He himself likes to beat us into bed
A man of the land with no control
Whippings with his walking stick
Then
Caught red handed with the billygoat
And then
Caught with the cousin and oh
The veteran landed blow on blow

You come to no harm
Just might grow dull and dumb
Holidays on the farm!

Erfurt

My father had a gun
He'd still be living
If only he'd not given
Me that gun

My mother too has passed
She'd still be living
If only she'd given
The abortionist a chance

And all my friends
Are dead and at rest
The kids and the teacher
I shot them in the chest

The smoke slowly clears
A whimpering a moan
A sad song sobs
An angel sings alone

The barrel deep between my teeth
Gives life after living
My father's gun
To the angel I've given

Under pressure

I've been under pressure
For days
Can't take your weight no more
You lie on me
So heavy
You've stopped getting up
Are you dead
Or have you just stopped living

Faust

Faust fist
Fistfight fisticuffs
Fistula Faustan
Fist pump fistfuck
Fausthaus ...

You can break with your fingers
But not with your hand balled
Get angry
Smash your fist into the wall

False Butterfly

Outside I am wicked pretty
But my soul is brimstone black
Red is for the morning dew
Poison green befits the lake
Oily blue for animals
But my black I keep for me
And all colours that I steal
From anyone who looks at me
I suck the colours from their eyes
And lock them in my soul to die

AIDS

He was a pilot
For a night
Flew away then
He expired

On Sunday I Must Die

I'm set to die on Sunday
But I'm going to scotch that by
Falling ill just wait and see
So I won't be able to die

Head High

Let me have a sniff
I said
Go ahead she said but be careful
I snuffled over the cover
The paper smelled of puke
We opened the book and looked into a train station

The train from Afar was running late
Had crashed off a bridge in Ten City but would now be
    coming via Linsolo
They told us
He took it every day from Hereonin via Lunt to Day and
    it was bound to happen
A Chinaman said
The bridge was temperamental the engine driver sad the
    tracks from Greenland Springy spring springs and
    then that happens
Said that Chinaman

We went back into the station
Zugzwang stress train
Got a drink and a Rolex from the dispenser for me and
    her and for
The journey and waited

Stations are full of people who never go anywhere
Drinking beer and shitting out tapeworms
Faces covered in blackheads
Some of them are very filthy

Others are fans of old fashion but
All give off a certain whiff
You never know what they're up to
They act very busy
Know the timetable and start to talk to you
If you get too close
Walk up and down busily
Like at a stock exchange

Now and then one gets arrested so badly
The yellow falls out of his hair

I went to the toilets on platform 8
But it's beyond me to report on that

The train came in and I felt better
Hands nicely washed
We said our farewells and I got on
There was tea and Mikado choccy biccies for all
I took my edelweiss handkerchief out of my pocket
And waved
Something crawled into my leg

Head High 2

I saw the face and flinched
So ugly
I hate mirrors

How can nature fail so badly
How can God be so blind
I don't believe it that's why I don't believe
God is nature
Nature is God and nature says no
Oh but can nobody see
Beneath my face
A beautiful heart races
Oh take me wild gusts of wind
From the fleshy sea of my sex
That no ship has yet sailed
God
Touch me
Spit your cascades
Upon my visage
Then I will pray for you
God
Make me handsome I will anoint bibles
Lick crosses
My soul let it be
A gift to you
For just some allure upon my mug
So I can use it for sexy delight
Seducing the gorgeous
Lovely ones nymphs

Who fondle only their equals
So give me them
And forgive me
For
I want them all

Head High 3

I'd been waving for a long while
My handkerchief was dry
The window was still open
I shut my eyes and let the wind go through my hair
It smelled of diesel
My shoulder ached
Then I stared at my shoes for a bit
Thought about my father
Not seen him for ages I thought
Died much too early
Of cancer
Outside knights in armour were jousting
and spearing each other's heads
One of them had got himself a superb skull
In celebration he wheeled his horse around
The dun failed to obey the reins
Its forelegs crumpled
The brave man went face first forwards
The lance swung around heavily
The head flew towards me
Swooped like a football
Through the compartment window
I caught it
He said thanks and asked if I'd eaten yet today
Then he shut his eyes and said nothing more
I'm a good eater
My stomach started rumbling like a guard dog
So I went to the dining car
Funny people those jousters

Toilet

At the request of a lady reader I can but
Truthfully report on the events
In the railway station toilet
But urge those of a sensitive disposition to skip these chapters

The shit house lay at the far end of the underpass below the platforms
I pushed my way past two guys my age with cunty beards
Smelling of mustard and asking me for change
There was no need to use the door handle
Missing
I shoved the door open and flinched
Biting stench
Never before had I breathed in the like
The door swung shut and it was dark tried to open it get some light in
And remembered the two scroungers just outside
Took my lighter from my trouser pocket and looked for the
    light switch
None there
Probably outside
Probably not a wet room switch or some reason like that
The two bums were still standing outside I could hear them grunting
I had my light and the stench had already stopped bothering me
There were three urinals one of which had been smashed to bits
The others were half
Full with a lady's handbag floating in one
I wondered what a bag snatcher makes in a day and if I should
Give it a try
I'd reached the squat boxes
The first cubicle was locked

Went to the next with uneasy anticipation
My breakfast was starting to get going
I hoped no one would come in now and see me in this treasure
    hunter posture
There was the bowl it was full to the brim though the flush
    seemed to be working
It splashed like a Harz mountain stream
I scanned the whole scene with expert eyes but gained no
    deeper insight
As with the light
I took off my coat which involved passing the lighter from one
    hand into my right hand
There wasn't a hook so I threw the coat over the door
With one hand I manoeuvred my belt open and lowered my pants
Taking care that no cloth touched the floor
Who knows what viruses and bacteria infest it and the textile'd
    be polluted
No doubt spurts of piss everywhere
The horror stories of parasite hosts
Held that dear flame downwards and looked about
Probably no one had been in here for days
All dry
A few fag ends a small patch of sick and half a grilled sausage
Looked around
On the walls were the usual scrawls
Who the hell has time whilst taking a shit to get a felt tip out of
    his jacket (who even carries a felt tip) and scribble cunts and
    pricks on the chipboard partitions plus telephone numbers
You'd first have to think them up
Or remember them from some antediluvian session in the
City park public conveniences
Suddenly there she was

My sunshine in the night
Hardly touched out of the darkness loomed the great white
Wound around with fifty-six meters of hymen
The virgin from hell
A roll of toilet paper
All would be well the lighter was getting hot
I took one step forwards just one so I'd return to the same spot
And not crap wide of the mark
Drew the coat towards me and dropped the lighter in a pocket
That one step taken back I crouched (sitting wasn't thinkable) and gave
In to sweet release unhurriedly

The muscle groups in the thigh which attach to the cruciate ligament
Only perform a supporting function for the knee joint and are not accustomed to
Longer-term load-bearing
They were hurting
I had to hurry up
I decided to wipe myself in the dark what could go wrong that happy roll
Was in feeling reach and the rest was routine
I unrolled a good two meters and like always made a six layer small strong pad
A fortress for my fingers
As I swung behind me the Rolex from the dispenser caught on a
Loop of the belt the strap broke and the watch slipped off my hand
Made a noise like when fillet falls onto the kitchen floor
I dropped the wipe pad and stood up
Felt for the coat to retrieve the lighter found the side pocket
And had my hand in a hornets nest
The zippo burned my fingers

Staggering in pain I reached for something to hold onto in the
    darkness
My radius of movement was highly restricted by the lowered
    pants
I lost my footing but managed to correct the fall in falling so I only
Struck the edge of the bowl with my shoulder and landed
Between shitpan and wall on the puke free side of the floor
I'd heard a loud crack like somebody snapping braces on naked
    skin
Cursing and shaking I rose to my feet again
On that floor I'd suffered the kiss of nausea I quickly pulled my
trousers up forgot about the bumwipe and the ignominy
Just wanted to see about the Rolex then get out of there
I pulled the ends of my pullover sleeves over my fingers found
    my coat and
Grabbed the lighter
I blew on it like on chicken soup
And now flick
Light
The impact of my shoulder had knocked one screw out of the
Anchoring of the ceramic base the lavatory was balancing
    precariously like a sinking boat
The other one was half out and bent
But was preventing the white dream from completely falling over
A major portion of its contents was spreading out over the tiles
I had one foot in faeces
I couldn't see the watch no doubt it had floated into the next cell
I rapidly exited the latrine
Stamped the shit from my shoe
Loads of it still sticking to the leather
Socks damp
Lighter hot again

I hastened to the washbasin stood the lighter in the empty soap
    tray and
Held my foot under the tap
I turned it expecting the worst
Water came
The flow was thin as a needle it was going to take forever
Before I'd even begin to get it clean
Besides I was still afraid somebody might come and
Fetch the police
The situation was desperate and urgent
I took off the shoe and chucked the sock in the general direction
    of the bog
Then I carefully fished the handkerchief embroidered with
    edelweiss out of my trouser pocket
Dipped the shoe into the pisser without the handbag and used
The handkerchief to wipe off the shit as best as I could in the
    fading light
(The fuel was running out) and put the shoe back on
Then I wrung out the hankie stuffed it into the shoe where else
Back to the sink
Washed my hands without soap as already mentioned none
    was there and found the
Light switch by the hand dryer but didn't try it
The two winos had gone
You took your time she said
I nodded and the train was announced I'd forgotten the lighter

Comfort

For creatures great and small the knowledge
When rain does lash and wind does roar
That the huntsman's staying indoors
By the fireside leaning back
Eating hot dogs from the pack
Getting his genitalia polished
Is a blessing to be relished

Mourning

I wear a black band on my arm
Not to look smart
It doesn't keep me warm
It keeps me shedding more tears
To people and to animals it says
Tristesse often runs on long legs

Candle

In my eyes burning sand
In her eyes tears of gasoline
The match falls from my hand

Mist

When the mist rises up from the meadows
I will cut open my skin
Two fathoms below my collarbone
Push the smooth steel in

And I will stab my eyes out
house without windows now
smash in my skull so the snow
snows in and my brain freezes down

And I will hack open my chest
so it rains and my heart gets wet
open up my veins with shears
present you a bunch of red tears

Every day I cut like from a sheet
of paper a piece off of me
lay them onto your head to get
them sinking inside your brain
to make me small so I can crawl
into your body domain

I'll climb up onto your breasts
and show myself the view
slip through your lips to kiss
your tongue is what I have to do

The mole on your leg will be my island
The little scar will be my nest

When you put on your dress so pale
I'll hold on tight to your tiny hairs and I'll cry tears
when you read a fairy tale

Red Ear

Behind your red ear
A black safe in your skin
Where your hair begins
A great big wart
With tiny treasure in
I slit it and let what's within
Uncurl unfurl
And fly away
To conquer the evil in the world

Heart theft

What have you done to me
Like a thief in the night
You boldly broke into my soul
Wanting to steal my life
Here take my heart just take it
I'm ruined anyway
Security lapse just take it
I gladly give my heart away
I lay it gently in your breast
Look after it kindly I request

Don't Turn Round

See I've brought you animals
From out the boggy ground
Remember oh I know you can
Their collars being found

Sing for me come sing
The kitten holds the ring
Dance for me come dance
See how the puppytail wags and wags

Don't be afraid
Don't be afraid of me
Don't turn round
I'm standing at your back
Turn turn
Around me
Turn around me turn around me turn around
But don't turn round

They're coming back again tonight
Out the greasy stove they spill
Animals we set alight
They're screaming cos they're burning still

Sing for me come sing
The kitten holds the ring
Dance for me come dance
See how the puppytail wags and wags

Don't be afraid
Don't be afraid of me
Don't turn round
I'm standing at your back
Turn turn
Around me
Turn around me turn around me turn around
But don't turn round

The Little Dog Wags Its Tail

Don't be afraid
Don't be afraid of me
Don't turn round
I'm standing at your back
Turn turn
Around me
Turn around me turn around me turn around
But don't turn round

Good night

Another day nearly gone
Darkness descending
Bids goodbye to daylight
Another day when I got nothing done
Who gives a shit
I'll do it tomorrow
Good night

Heartfelt and Soul

I dropped the baby on the floor
It twitched a bit
A little blood
A tiny tear falls down on Daddy's
Shag pile rug
Heartfelt and soul
Kid's still alive
Mom's gotta heave
With hurt and soul
Good luck
And bad
Bye bye

Oh with Delight

I've known a lot of lovely ladies
In this lovely world
A ladies man yes that's the way we
Like to say it—I get called

Shameless, lacking decency
Heartless, loveless, frivolous
They say I forced them—let me see
The truth is more ambiguous

Oh with delight I women kissed
Nor only on the mouth indeed
I had to find out how they taste
And kissed until my lips did bleed

The cheeks I kissed weren't only pink
I just adored each every double
They say my lust's a fetid sink
Obsessive is my urge to couple

They say I'm drowning in a mire
They say my lust's a fetid sink
Of sick libidinous desire
It's a point of view—here's what I think

Oh with delight I women kissed
Nor only on the mouth indeed
I had to find out how they taste
And kissed until my lips did bleed

114

I simply took them in my arms
And if they gently sighed "please no"
I'd show no mercy with their charms
And make them wish they'd not been so

Rabbit-like when my great snake
My chilly eye, my sudden strike
My venomous desire to slake
Took me over, and the like.

Oh the women, loyal, oh so
Broken hearted some they were
Yes they'd wish they hadn't been so
Tearful screaming flying fur

Oh with delight I women kissed
Nor only on the mouth indeed
I had to find out how they taste
And kissed until my lips did bleed

Simply took them in my arms
If they gently sighed "please no"
Showed no mercy with their charms
Made them happy don't you know

No Further Down

No
No further
No further down
No further down to fall
Just stagger and babble and crawl

I've no further down to sink
Not much more I can drink
I can't snort much more
Sweaty chilly slaphead
All because that stupid cow
My puke choking me now

Won't let anybody see
How far down she's brought me
Tears like rivers streaming
My smile keeps on beaming

Short life

Life is so short
The sun's purported
To be forever
Life comes about
And it comes on
Then you come along
Little else comes up

Yesterday

Is dead
Today stinks
And as for tomorrow
I don't give a shit

Getter

He gets them laughing
He gets them drinks
He gets her interested
Soon he gets her home
He gets her crying
Then he gets her dead

Stay

Lying quiet in my arms
irresistible charms
stained with wild kisses
my good old pillow

Banana

Everybody loves bananas
Not so much dogs but children do
Everyone loves bananas
Monkeys do and women do too

Everybody loves bananas
Everybody in the world
All the women and the monkeys
Everybody loves bananas
From China back to the Bahamas

Ballet

And then she dances over air
And then she spreads her legs wide
And then I catch the scent of her
And silently break down and cry

Pure Fun

I'm not going to have any fun
Except for loving you any more
Loving you you can be sure
More and more is my only fun

Seamstress

What's a girl who cuts herself
Who takes a razor to her veins
In German she's a seamstress
Cutting's much more than a game

Seamstress seamstress listen up
In your body leave your blood
Take no razor to your veins
My word
Things will get better again

What's a boy who cuts himself
Who takes a razor to his veins
In German he's a basket case
Cutting's much more than a game

Letting blood's more than enough
The brain is bursting with the stuff
Drop your arms relax be cool
Hey you
Things won't get better you fool

Death by Animals

It happens
You can
Get killed
By an animal
This is horrific and brutal
For
The person who dies
Goes through agonies
Because often the animals
After catching you
Really take their time
Over dispatching you
That's why I hope
That neither by land nor by sea
May an animal be what kills me

Lion

The lion eats and here's a lean
And hungry hanging round hyena
Waiting for the king of beasts
To leave remains on which she feasts

Laughing is Good for You

The hole in the middle of your phiz
is a mouth, it's for talking with
of course it's for coughing and gasping and gassing
you can do even more
with it sure
but a mouth's also good for laughing

That's the hole you make noise through like laughing
laughing is good for you
It's the hole in the middle of your phiz for laughing
animal laughter don't exist

Animals they have it good
Only worries sex and food
Never needing to explain
Never asked to. Whooping crane,
Manatee, narwhal, orca, pike,
Zebra, cobra or giraffe
Tell them all the jokes you like
Never will you get a laugh

Second Place

I thank me
For my good deeds
Even if they didn't
Always please
I thank me
For my efforts
No one's achieved
More ever

It's a known fact
I race at the front of the pack
But one day I suddenly knew
First place isn't always you
Sometimes second place must do
Second place is pretty good too

Short

Short nose
Short life
Short pause
Short strife
Short game
And short shine
Short shrift
But oh dear
Oh dear oh no
Short penis, oh dear son
Short trousers, toy gun

Small Spoon Big Belly

I thought it was bigger
But it was only small
So much to say
But said nothing at all
Magic's no better
When a wand is lengthy
What use a big spoon
When my dish is empty

Now You Are Dead

Now you are dead
I have a future
Nothingness
Is now your suitor
One dies the other has a life
What could be cuter

I only came to see you
Buried in the ground
A man all dressed in black
Is arsing around
God's blessing he goes on about
Now you are dead
Your life is out

I have a future
The mourners stand and whine
The widow I'm her suitor
Just fucked her fine
Sobbing in her black dress
What display of sadness
You are dead
I've no regrets

You

I wanna be you
That'd be cool
I could pass all me time
Stroking me titties relaxin
No more longin glances
No smears an spatter
No lickin dust off a platter
To ell wi all me brood
Even me grammar'd be good
An rich too
Beautiful
Just on an off
Go work
Be all art and culture vulture like
Me bidet no more full of shite
I wanna be you
Round the clock
An if your fella
Stops givin me cock
I can sleep wi the collie
So what
Others do it wi sheep
Mine does it to me
The swine
Falls asleep on top of me
An since you brung it up I wanna be you
And your kid too
Tie er pigtails every day
Answer whatever she asks away

Welp'll be well off wi me
Stead of beltins I give er beer
Them as says it's bad for yer health
Rubbish just look at meself
Neckin schnaps at the age of twelf
Never did me no harm
True me father did rape me I spose
But I dint complain as it goes
Every man has urges he can't control
I'm alive still
Thank god
But I reckon I'm kinda gross somehow
So I wish I was like you right now
But I kinda get too
No way I can never be you

Somehow

It's all gonna somehow work out fine
But somehow this is really wrong
Life never said thanks too much to ask?
All you have to do is walk straight on
Look into the chasm with a steady glance
So that's the way you thank me now
Yes this is paying back and how
I'm up here on the mountainside
Looking down on you as you die

Coffee

I like a cup of coffee
I like the taste
It keeps me awake
When the sun goes down
That's when
I have a cup of coffee
With a lot of milk
And sugar too
To give me a kick
And when the night falls
That's when
I'm really pumped up
And that's when I fuck

Little Voice

Send me please a word or two
Your lovely mouth I beg you I adore
is it asking much too much to
Let me hear your little voice once more

Flayed amid the flames beseeching
Let me feel your little voice
You can soothe me just by speaking
My scorching heart your words anoint

When tears are lashing me by night
My flesh torn open everywhere
Your speech has the might
To make the horror fair

Second Skin

You
Are my second skin
Always there
Close by
So close by
I breathe through you
Smell you
Damp
You're my second blood
And it's on fire

You'll Die Soon

He:
You drink
You smoke
You take drugs
You constantly cheat on your wife
You're revolting you're unhealthy
You're shortening your life

You drink you smoke
You take drugs
Every woman in your life you've lied to
The way you live is round the bend
Disgusting and vile and woe betide you
You're heading towards an untimely end

Me:
Listen up
I can give
Reasons for the way I live
Fact is sick things
And getting messed
Happen to be what brings
Most happiness
Better brief and intense
Than a life of dreary length
Better drugs and excess
Than life that's long but jestless
I my friend am far from sad
Enjoyed every breath I've taken

When the time comes I'll go glad
Not one thing I'm
Regretting
Booze and fucking whores and fun's
Better than a long life sentence
Of staring at my reflection

Photo: Bryan Adams

About the Author

Till Lindemann was born in 1963 in Leipzig, the son of children's book author and writer Werner Lindemann and journalist Brigitta Lindemann. In his youth he was a competitive swimmer and was in line to go to the 1980 Olympics in Moscow but an injury ended his participation in the sport. He worked as an apprentice carpenter, a gallery technician, a peat cutter and a basket weaver. In 1994 he became singer and lyricist for Rammstein. He lives in Berlin. His first book of poems, *Messer*, was published in 2005. Another collection, *In stillen Nächten*, was released in 2013. *100 Poems* was orginally published as *100 Gedichte* in Germany in 2020.

Made in the USA
Columbia, SC
06 August 2025

2f175a5c-f0ff-4d69-bccd-e5c5277295c1R01